Tattoo
LETTERING
INSPIRATION
REFERENCE
Book

·VOLUME 1·

BLACKLETTER,
CALIGRAPHY,
CHOLO SCRIPT
& FLOURISHES

EDITIONS Vault

TATTOO LETTERING: A BRIEF INTRODUCTION

Although it's hard to pinpoint precisely when the first lettering tattoos were produced, we know that it wasn't until the 1700s that Western society began to adopt tattoos into their culture. According to historical records, sailors were among the first to get tattooed, notably the crew aboard Captain James Cook's ship. They collected tattoos throughout their voyages as mementoes of their adventures from nations with a long lineage of tattoo cultures, such as Japan, New Zealand and the Pacific Islands. As the pictorial tapestry of tattoo culture began to develop, both sailors and military service members would receive iconographic tattoos emblazoned with names of loved ones, symbolic homeland reminders, as well as words steeped in courage, dedication or brotherhood.

Fast-forward to today, and tattoos have gained popularity exponentially. Approximately 30% of men and women in the United States have at least one tattoo, many of them being purely typographic. The taboo stigma of tattoos only being for criminals, gangs and punks is now over, and the culture has rocketed into the mainstream. One thing remains steadfast; a typographic tattoo is a profoundly personal addition to one's body and requires a high level of dedication to sit through the painful process. They can be a memento to commemorate the passing of a loved one, a symbolic reminder to take courage in challenging times, or an honourary tribute to new life or new beginnings.

INTRODUCTION

The Tattoo Lettering Inspiration Reference Book is a resource of tattoo inspired typefaces to help take your tattoo lettering and hand lettering designs to the next level. The typefaces featured within this book are crafted by leading type designers, including Muntab Art, Creativemedialab and RVQ Type Foundry. This book highlights a diverse and comprehensive range of blackletter fonts, ornamental scripts, west coast and calligraphic alphabets, as well as flourishes and filigree.

ACCESS YOUR FREE DOWNLOADS

Downloading your files is simple. To access your digital files, please go to the last page of this book and follow the instructions.

For technical assistance, please email:
info@vaulteditions.com

Copyright
Copyright © Vault Editions Ltd 2020.

Bibliographical Note

This book is a new work created by Vault Editions Ltd.

ISBN: 978-1-925968-70-5

TATTOO LETTERING

VAULT EDITIONS

.PRACTICE.
SHEET

.TATTOO.
Lettering Reference

.TYPEFACE.
EASTSIDE

DISPALY SIZE: 50ᴾᵀ ⟷ WEIGHT: REGULAR ⟷ LEADING: 74ᴾᵀ

1

LEARN MORE ABOUT THE DESIGNER

WEBSITE: MUNTABART.COM
INSTAGRAM: MUNTAB_ART

© MUNTAB ART

VOLUME №1

VAULTEDITIONS.COM

.DESIGNER.
MUNTAB ART

.TATTOO.
Lettering Reference

.TYPEFACE.
EASTSIDE

DISPALY SIZE: 90ᴾᵀ   ⟷   WEIGHT: REGULAR   ⟷   LEADING: 74ᴾᵀ

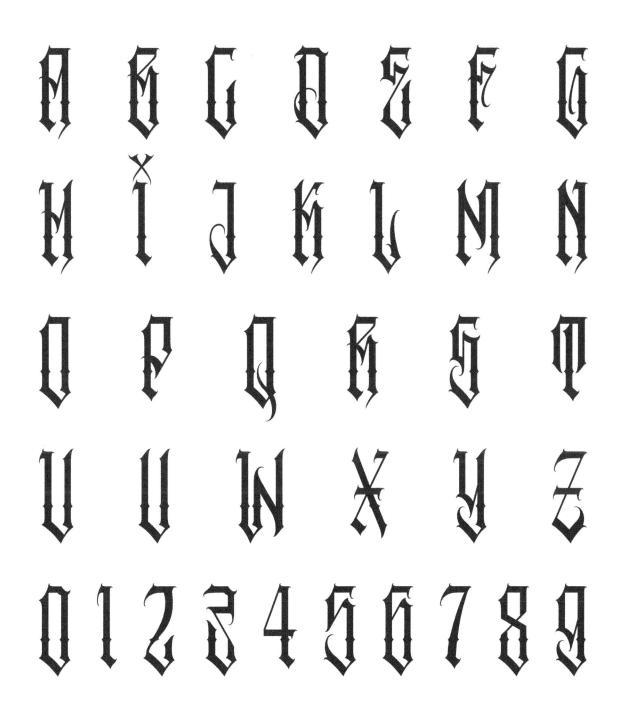

2

LEARN MORE ABOUT
THE DESIGNER

WEBSITE: MUNTABART.COM
INSTAGRAM: MUNTAB_ART

© MUNTAB ART   VOLUME №1

VAULTEDITIONS.COM

.PRACTICE.
SHEET

.TATTOO.
Lettering Reference

.TYPEFACE.
BANDITO

DISPALY SIZE: 50ᴾᵀ ⟷ WEIGHT: REGULAR ⟷ LEADING: 74ᴾᵀ

3

LEARN MORE ABOUT
THE DESIGNER

WEBSITE: MUNTABART.COM
INSTAGRAM: MUNTAB_ART

© MUNTAB ART | VOLUME №1

VAULTEDITIONS.COM

.DESIGNER.
MUNTAB ART

.TATTOO.
Lettering Reference

.TYPEFACE.
BANDITO

DISPALY SIZE: 72^{PT} ←→ **WEIGHT: REGULAR** ←→ **LEADING: 74^{PT}**

4

LEARN MORE ABOUT
THE DESIGNER

WEBSITE: MUNTABART.COM
INSTAGRAM: MUNTAB_ART

© MUNTAB ART | VOLUME №1

VAULTEDITIONS.COM

.PRACTICE.
SHEET

.TATTOO.
Lettering Reference

.TYPEFACE.
BANDITO SWASH

DISPALY SIZE: 50ᴾᵀ ⟵ ⟶ **WEIGHT: REGULAR** ⟵ ⟶ **LEADING: 74ᴾᵀ**

LEARN MORE ABOUT
THE DESIGNER

WEBSITE: MUNTABART.COM
INSTAGRAM: MUNTAB_ART

© MUNTAB ART | VOLUME №1

VAULTEDITIONS.COM

.DESIGNER.
MUNTAB ART

.TATTOO.
LETTERING REFERENCE

.TYPEFACE.
BANDITO SWASH

DISPALY SIZE: 60ᴾᵀ ⟷ WEIGHT: REGULAR ⟷ LEADING: 74ᴾᵀ

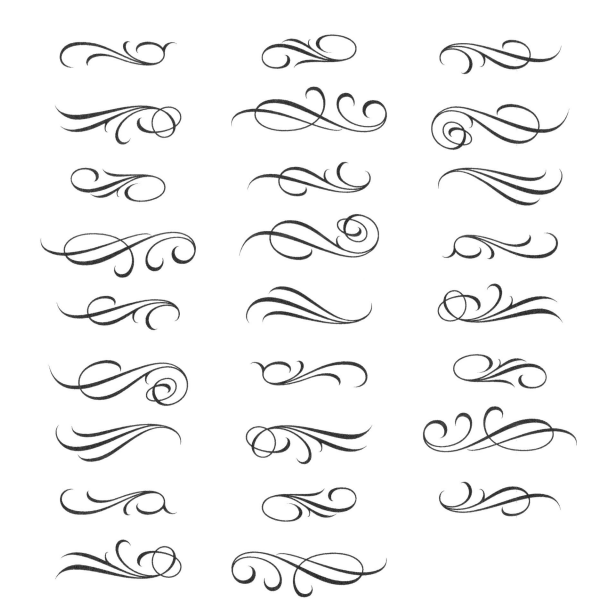

6

LEARN MORE ABOUT
THE DESIGNER

WEBSITE: MUNTABART.COM
INSTAGRAM: MUNTAB_ART

© MUNTAB ART

VOLUME №1

VAULTEDITIONS.COM

.PRACTICE.
SHEET

.TATTOO.
Lettering Reference

.TYPEFACE.
SOUTHSIDE

DISPALY SIZE: 50PT ←→ **WEIGHT: REGULAR** ←→ **LEADING: 74**PT

**LEARN MORE ABOUT
THE DESIGNER**

**WEBSITE: MUNTABART.COM
INSTAGRAM: MUNTAB_ART**

© MUNTAB ART | **VOLUME №1**

VAULTEDITIONS.COM

.DESIGNER.
MUNTAB ART

.TATTOO.
Lettering Reference

.TYPEFACE.
SOUTHSIDE

DISPALY SIZE: 89^{PT} ← → WEIGHT: REGULAR ← → LEADING: 74^{PT}

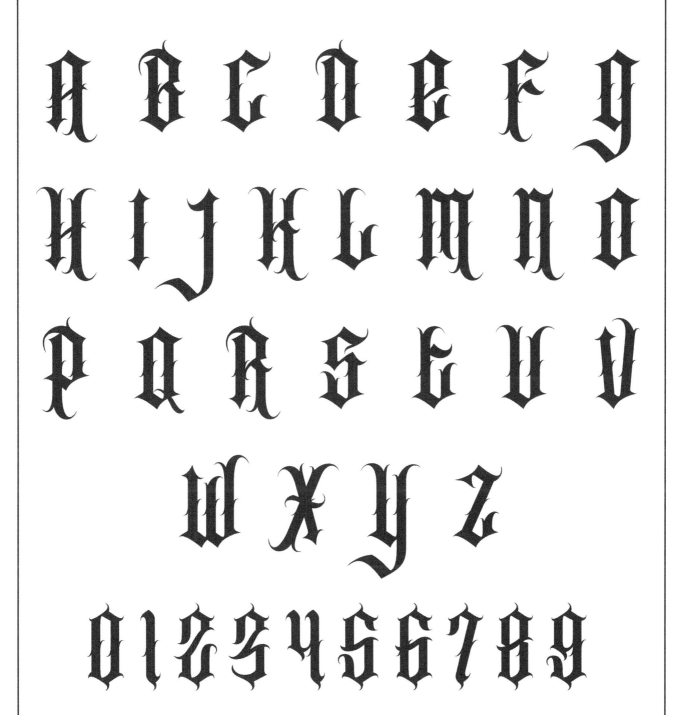

8

LEARN MORE ABOUT
THE DESIGNER

WEBSITE: MUNTABART.COM
INSTAGRAM: MUNTAB_ART

CREATION AND RESTORATION SERVICES CURATION

© MUNTAB ART | VOLUME №1

VAULTEDITIONS.COM

.PRACTICE.
SHEET

.TATTOO.
Lettering Reference

.TYPEFACE.
TRIBAL

DISPALY SIZE: 50PT	WEIGHT: REGULAR	LEADING: 74PT

LEARN MORE ABOUT THE DESIGNER	WEBSITE: MUNTABART.COM INSTAGRAM: MUNTAB_ART		© MUNTAB ART	VOLUME №1
			VAULTEDITIONS.COM	

CURATION AND RESTORATION SERVICES

·DESIGNER·
MUNTAB ART

·TATTOO·
Lettering Reference

·TYPEFACE·
TRIBAL

10

LEARN MORE ABOUT
THE DESIGNER

WEBSITE: MUNTABART.COM
INSTAGRAM: MUNTAB_ART

© MUNTAB ART

VOLUME №1

VAULTEDITIONS.COM

.PRACTICE.
SHEET

.TATTOO.
Lettering Reference

.TYPEFACE.
GANGSTA

DISPALY SIZE: 50^{PT} ⟷   WEIGHT: REGULAR   ⟷   LEADING: 74^{PT}

LEARN MORE ABOUT
THE DESIGNER

WEBSITE: MUNTABART.COM
INSTAGRAM: MUNTAB_ART

© MUNTAB ART   VOLUME №1

VAULTEDITIONS.COM

.DESIGNER.
MUNTAB ART

.TATTOO.
Lettering Reference

.TYPEFACE.
GANGSTA

DISPALY SIZE: 60ᴾᵀ ⟷ **WEIGHT: REGULAR** ⟷ **LEADING: 74ᴾᵀ**

.PRACTICE.
SHEET

.TATTOO.
Lettering Reference

.TYPEFACE.
GANGSTA ITALIC

DISPALY SIZE: 50PT ⟷ **WEIGHT: REGULAR** ⟷ **LEADING: 74PT**

13

LEARN MORE ABOUT
THE DESIGNER

WEBSITE: MUNTABART.COM
INSTAGRAM: MUNTAB_ART

© MUNTAB ART | VOLUME №1

VAULTEDITIONS.COM

.DESIGNER.
MUNTAB ART

.TATTOO.
Lettering Reference

.TYPEFACE.
GANGSTA ITALIC

DISPALY SIZE: 60PT   ⟷   WEIGHT: REGULAR   ⟷   LEADING: 74PT

14

LEARN MORE ABOUT
THE DESIGNER

WEBSITE: MUNTABART.COM
INSTAGRAM: MUNTAB_ART

© MUNTAB ART   VOLUME №1

VAULTEDITIONS.COM

.PRACTICE.
SHEET

.TATTOO.
Lettering Reference

.TYPEFACE.
GANGSTA SWASH

DISPALY SIZE: 50PT ⟷ **WEIGHT: REGULAR** ⟷ **LEADING: 74**PT

LEARN MORE ABOUT
THE DESIGNER

WEBSITE: MUNTABART.COM
INSTAGRAM: MUNTAB_ART

CURATION AND RESTORATION SERVICES

© MUNTAB ART   VOLUME №1

VAULTEDITIONS.COM

.DESIGNER.
MUNTAB ART

.TATTOO.
Lettering Reference

.TYPEFACE.
GANGSTA SWASH

DISPALY SIZE: 50ᴾᵀ ⟷ WEIGHT: REGULAR ⟷ LEADING: 74ᴾᵀ

LEARN MORE ABOUT
THE DESIGNER

WEBSITE: MUNTABART.COM
INSTAGRAM: MUNTAB_ART

© MUNTAB ART | VOLUME №1

VAULTEDITIONS.COM

.PRACTICE.
SHEET

.TATTOO.
Lettering Reference

.TYPEFACE.
CHICANO

DISPALY SIZE: 50^{PT} ⟷ **WEIGHT: REGULAR** ⟷ **LEADING: 74^{PT}**

17

LEARN MORE ABOUT
THE DESIGNER

WEBSITE: MUNTABART.COM
INSTAGRAM: MUNTAB_ART

© MUNTAB ART

VOLUME №1

VAULTEDITIONS.COM

.DESIGNER.
MUNTAB ART

.TATTOO.
Lettering Reference

.TYPEFACE.
CHICANO

18

LEARN MORE ABOUT
THE DESIGNER

WEBSITE: MUNTABART.COM
INSTAGRAM: MUNTAB_ART

© MUNTAB ART

VOLUME №1

VAULTEDITIONS.COM

.PRACTICE.
SHEET

.TATTOO.
Lettering Reference

.TYPEFACE.
FAMILIA

DISPALY SIZE: 50ᴾᵀ ← → **WEIGHT: REGULAR** ← → **LEADING: 74ᴾᵀ**

LEARN MORE ABOUT
THE DESIGNER

WEBSITE: MUNTABART.COM
INSTAGRAM: MUNTAB_ART

© MUNTAB ART | VOLUME №1

VAULTEDITIONS.COM

· DESIGNER ·
MUNTAB ART

· TATTOO ·
Lettering Reference

· TYPEFACE ·
FAMILIA

DISPALY SIZE: 50ᴾᵀ ⟷ WEIGHT: REGULAR ⟷ LEADING: 74ᴾᵀ

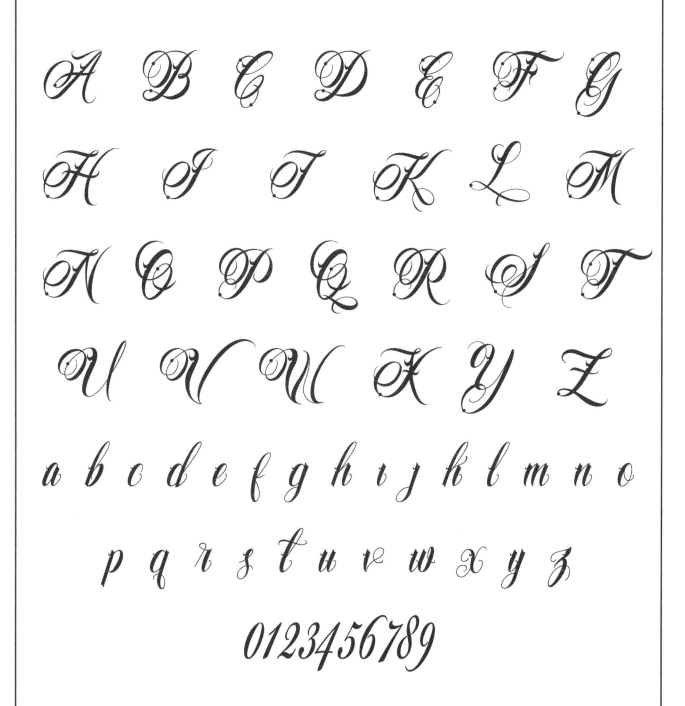

20

LEARN MORE ABOUT
THE DESIGNER

WEBSITE: MUNTABART.COM
INSTAGRAM: MUNTAB_ART

© MUNTAB ART | VOLUME №1

VAULTEDITIONS.COM

.PRACTICE.
SHEET

.TATTOO.
Lettering Reference

.TYPEFACE.
CHICANO VOL.02

DISPALY SIZE: 50ᴾᵀ ← → **WEIGHT: REGULAR** ← → **LEADING: 74ᴾᵀ**

21

LEARN MORE ABOUT
THE DESIGNER

WEBSITE: MUNTABART.COM
INSTAGRAM: MUNTAB_ART

CURATION AND RESTORATION SERVICES

© MUNTAB ART | VOLUME №1

VAULTEDITIONS.COM

.DESIGNER.
MUNTAB ART

.TATTOO.
LETTERING REFERENCE

.TYPEFACE.
CHICANO VOL.02

DISPALY SIZE: 50ᴾᵀ ⟷ **WEIGHT: REGULAR** ⟷ **LEADING: 74ᴾᵀ**

22

LEARN MORE ABOUT
THE DESIGNER

WEBSITE: MUNTABART.COM
INSTAGRAM: MUNTAB_ART

© MUNTAB ART   VOLUME №1

VAULTEDITIONS.COM

.PRACTICE.
SHEET

.TATTOO.
Lettering Reference

.TYPEFACE.
CHICANO VOL.02
SWASH

DISPALY SIZE: 50ᴾᵀ ←——→ WEIGHT: REGULAR ←——→ LEADING: 74ᴾᵀ

LEARN MORE ABOUT
THE DESIGNER

WEBSITE: MUNTABART.COM
INSTAGRAM: MUNTAB_ART

CURATION AND RESTORATION SERVICES

© MUNTAB ART

VOLUME №1

VAULTEDITIONS.COM

.DESIGNER.
MUNTAB ART

.TATTOO.
LETTERING REFERENCE

.TYPEFACE.
CHICANO VOL.02
SWASH

DISPALY SIZE: 50ᴾᵀ ⟷   WEIGHT: REGULAR   ⟷   LEADING: 48ᴾᵀ

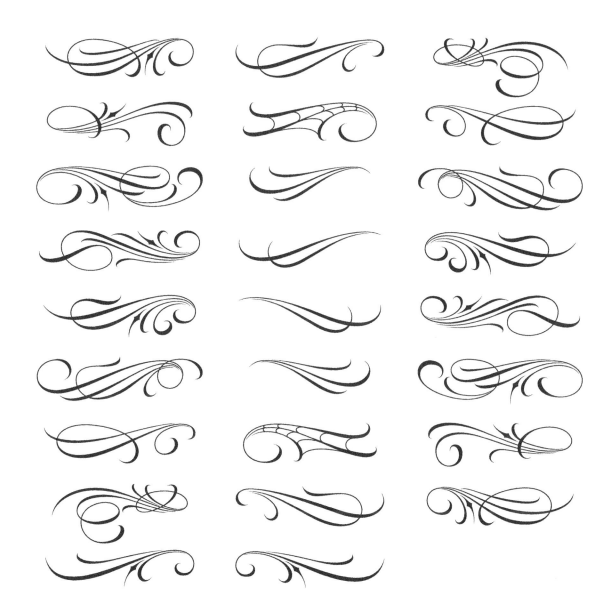

LEARN MORE ABOUT
THE DESIGNER

WEBSITE: MUNTABART.COM
INSTAGRAM: MUNTAB_ART

© MUNTAB ART   VOLUME №1

VAULTEDITIONS.COM

.PRACTICE.
SHEET

.TATTOO.
Lettering Reference

.TYPEFACE.
DAYLES

DISPALY SIZE: 50PT   ←——→   **WEIGHT: REGULAR**   ←——→   **LEADING: 74**PT

25

LEARN MORE ABOUT
THE DESIGNER

WEBSITE: MUNTABART.COM
INSTAGRAM: MUNTAB_ART

© MUNTAB ART   VOLUME №1

VAULTEDITIONS.COM

.DESIGNER.
MUNTAB ART

.TATTOO.
Lettering Reference

.TYPEFACE.
DAYLES

DISPALY SIZE: 50PT ← → WEIGHT: REGULAR ← → LEADING: 74PT

26

LEARN MORE ABOUT
THE DESIGNER

WEBSITE: MUNTABART.COM
INSTAGRAM: MUNTAB_ART

© MUNTAB ART | VOLUME №1

VAULTEDITIONS.COM

. PRACTICE .

SHEET

. TATTOO .

Lettering Reference

. TYPEFACE .

MALDITO

DISPALY SIZE: 50PT ← → **WEIGHT: REGULAR** ← → **LEADING: 74**PT

LEARN MORE ABOUT
THE DESIGNER

WEBSITE: MUNTABART.COM
INSTAGRAM: MUNTAB_ART

SERVICES CURATION AND RESTORATION

© MUNTAB ART

VOLUME №1

VAULTEDITIONS.COM

.DESIGNER.
MUNTAB ART

.TATTOO.
Lettering Reference

.TYPEFACE.
MALDITO

DISPALY SIZE: 50ᴾᵀ ⟷ WEIGHT: REGULAR ⟷ LEADING: 74ᴾᵀ

28

LEARN MORE ABOUT
THE DESIGNER

WEBSITE: MUNTABART.COM
INSTAGRAM: MUNTAB_ART

CURATION AND RESTORATION SERVICES

© MUNTAB ART | VOLUME №1

VAULTEDITIONS.COM

.PRACTICE.
SHEET

.TATTOO.
Lettering Reference

.TYPEFACE.
MALDITO SWASH

DISPALY SIZE: 50ᴾᵀ ⟷ WEIGHT: REGULAR ⟷ LEADING: 74ᴾᵀ

29

LEARN MORE ABOUT
THE DESIGNER

WEBSITE: MUNTABART.COM
INSTAGRAM: MUNTAB_ART

© MUNTAB ART | VOLUME №1

VAULTEDITIONS.COM

.DESIGNER.
MUNTAB ART

.TATTOO.
Lettering Reference

.TYPEFACE.
MALDITO SWASH

DISPALY SIZE: 61ᴾᵀ ⟵ ⟶ **WEIGHT: REGULAR** ⟵ ⟶ **LEADING: 74ᴾᵀ**

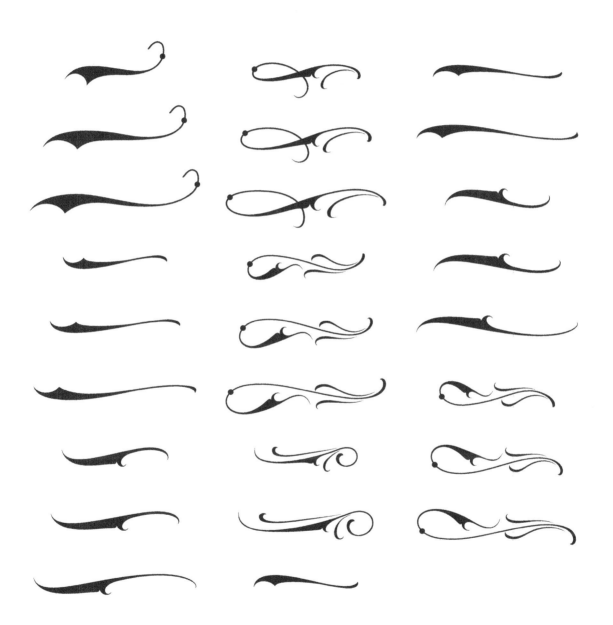

LEARN MORE ABOUT
THE DESIGNER

WEBSITE: MUNTABART.COM
INSTAGRAM: MUNTAB_ART

© MUNTAB ART   VOLUME №1

VAULTEDITIONS.COM

.PRACTICE.
SHEET

.TATTOO.
LETTERING REFERENCE

.TYPEFACE.
BABYLON

DISPALY SIZE: 50ᴾᵀ ← → **WEIGHT: REGULAR** ← → **LEADING: 74ᴾᵀ**

31

LEARN MORE ABOUT
THE DESIGNER

WEBSITE: MUNTABART.COM
INSTAGRAM: MUNTAB_ART

© MUNTAB ART | VOLUME №1

VAULTEDITIONS.COM

·DESIGNER·
MUNTAB ART

·TATTOO·
LETTERING REFERENCE

·TYPEFACE·
BABYLON

DISPALY SIZE: 72ᴾᵀ ⟷ WEIGHT: REGULAR ⟷ LEADING: 74ᴾᵀ

32

LEARN MORE ABOUT
THE DESIGNER

WEBSITE: MUNTABART.COM
INSTAGRAM: MUNTAB_ART

© MUNTAB ART | VOLUME №1

VAULTEDITIONS.COM

.PRACTICE.
SHEET

.TATTOO.
Lettering Reference

.TYPEFACE.
PLEASURE

DISPALY SIZE: 50ᴾᵀ ←——→ WEIGHT: REGULAR ←——→ LEADING: 74ᴾᵀ

.DESIGNER.
MUNTAB ART

.TATTOO.
Lettering Reference

.TYPEFACE.
PLEASURE

DISPALY SIZE: 75^{PT} ←→ WEIGHT: REGULAR ←→ LEADING: 74^{PT}

A B C D E F G
H I J K L M N
O P Q R S T U
V W X Y Z

a b c d e f g h i j k l m n o p

q r s t u v w x y z

0 1 2 3 4 5 6 7 8 9

. PRACTICE .

SHEET

. TATTOO .

Lettering Reference

. TYPEFACE .

MINERVA

DISPALY SIZE: 50^{PT} ← → **WEIGHT: REGULAR** ← → **LEADING: 74^{PT}**

35

LEARN MORE ABOUT
THE DESIGNER

WEBSITE: MUNTABART.COM
INSTAGRAM: MUNTAB_ART

© MUNTAB ART | VOLUME №1

VAULTEDITIONS.COM

.DESIGNER.
MUNTAB ART

.TATTOO.
Lettering Reference

.TYPEFACE.
MINERVA

DISPALY SIZE: 91ᴾᵀ ⟷ WEIGHT: REGULAR ⟷ LEADING: 74ᴾᵀ

36

LEARN MORE ABOUT
THE DESIGNER

WEBSITE: MUNTABART.COM
INSTAGRAM: MUNTAB_ART

© MUNTAB ART | VOLUME №1

VAULTEDITIONS.COM

.PRACTICE.
SHEET

.TATTOO.
Lettering Reference

.TYPEFACE.
MARTYR

DISPALY SIZE: 50^{PT} ← → **WEIGHT: REGULAR** ← → **LEADING: 74^{PT}**

37

LEARN MORE ABOUT
THE DESIGNER

WEBSITE: MUNTABART.COM
INSTAGRAM: MUNTAB_ART

© MUNTAB ART | VOLUME №1

VAULTEDITIONS.COM

· DESIGNER ·
MUNTAB ART

· TATTOO ·
LETTERING REFERENCE

· TYPEFACE ·
MARTYR

DISPALY SIZE: 72ᴾᵀ ⟷ WEIGHT: REGULAR ⟷ LEADING: 74ᴾᵀ

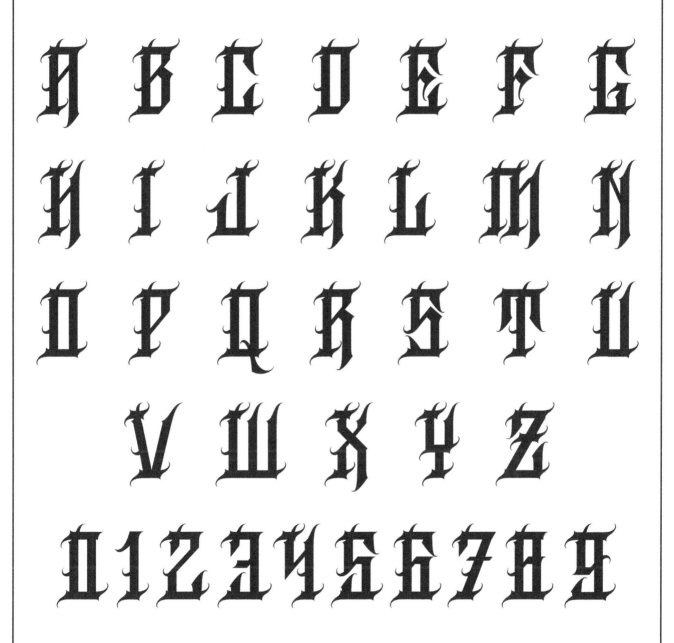

38

LEARN MORE ABOUT
THE DESIGNER

WEBSITE: MUNTABART.COM
INSTAGRAM: MUNTAB_ART

© MUNTAB ART   VOLUME №1

VAULTEDITIONS.COM

.PRACTICE.
SHEET

.TATTOO.
Lettering Reference

.TYPEFACE.
CHICANO VOL.02

DISPALY SIZE: 50ᴾᵀ ← → **WEIGHT: REGULAR** ← → **LEADING: 74ᴾᵀ**

LEARN MORE ABOUT
THE DESIGNER

WEBSITE: MUNTABART.COM
INSTAGRAM: MUNTAB_ART

© MUNTAB ART — VOLUME №1

VAULTEDITIONS.COM

.DESIGNER.
MUNTAB ART

.TATTOO.
Lettering Reference

.TYPEFACE.
SOUTHSIDE ORNAMENT

DISPALY SIZE: 50ᴾᵀ ⟷ WEIGHT: REGULAR ⟷ LEADING: 74ᴾᵀ

LEARN MORE ABOUT
THE DESIGNER

WEBSITE: MUNTABART.COM
INSTAGRAM: MUNTAB_ART

CURATION AND RESTORATION SERVICES

© MUNTAB ART

VOLUME №1

VAULTEDITIONS.COM

. PRACTICE .

SHEET

. TATTOO .

Lettering Reference

. TYPEFACE .

MAYHEM

DISPALY SIZE: 50ᴾᵀ ⟷ **WEIGHT: REGULAR** ⟷ **LEADING: 74ᴾᵀ**

41

LEARN MORE ABOUT
THE DESIGNER

WEBSITE: MUNTABART.COM
INSTAGRAM: MUNTAB_ART

© MUNTAB ART | VOLUME №1

VAULTEDITIONS.COM

.DESIGNER.
MUNTAB ART

.TATTOO.
Lettering Reference

.TYPEFACE.
MAYHEM

DISPALY SIZE: 104ᴾᵀ ⟷ **WEIGHT: REGULAR** ⟷ **LEADING: 74ᴾᵀ**

A B C D E F G

H I J K L M N

O P Q R S T

U V W X Y Z

0 1 2 3 4 5 6 7 8 9

LEARN MORE ABOUT
THE DESIGNER

WEBSITE: MUNTABART.COM
INSTAGRAM: MUNTAB_ART

SERVICES CURATION AND RESTORATION

© MUNTAB ART | VOLUME №1

VAULTEDITIONS.COM

.PRACTICE.
SHEET

.TATTOO.
Lettering Reference

.TYPEFACE.
SANTIAGO

DISPALY SIZE: 50ᴾᵀ ←→ **WEIGHT: REGULAR** ←→ **LEADING: 74ᴾᵀ**

43

LEARN MORE ABOUT
THE DESIGNER

WEBSITE: MUNTABART.COM
INSTAGRAM: MUNTAB_ART

CORATTIO AND RESTORATION
SERVICES CORATTIO

© MUNTAB ART | VOLUME №1

VAULTEDITIONS.COM

.DESIGNER.
MUNTAB ART

.TATTOO.
Lettering Reference

.TYPEFACE.
SANTIAGO

DISPALY SIZE: 101ᴾᵀ ⟷ **WEIGHT: REGULAR** ⟷ **LEADING: 74ᴾᵀ**

44

LEARN MORE ABOUT
THE DESIGNER

WEBSITE: MUNTABART.COM
INSTAGRAM: MUNTAB_ART

© MUNTAB ART | VOLUME №1

VAULTEDITIONS.COM

. PRACTICE .

SHEET

. TATTOO .

Lettering Reference

. TYPEFACE .

MACRON

DISPALY SIZE: 50PT ⟵ ⟶ **WEIGHT: REGULAR** ⟵ ⟶ **LEADING: 74**PT

45

LEARN MORE ABOUT
THE DESIGNER

WEBSITE: MUNTABART.COM
INSTAGRAM: MUNTAB_ART

© MUNTAB ART | VOLUME №1

VAULTEDITIONS.COM

·DESIGNER·
MUNTAB ART

·TATTOO·
Lettering Reference

·TYPEFACE·
MACRON

DISPALY SIZE: 73ᴾᵀ ⟷   WEIGHT: REGULAR   ⟷ LEADING: 74ᴾᵀ

A B C D E F G

H I J K L M N

O P Q R S T

U V W X Y Z

0 1 2 3 4 5 6 7 8 9

46

LEARN MORE ABOUT
THE DESIGNER

WEBSITE: MUNTABART.COM
INSTAGRAM: MUNTAB_ART

© MUNTAB ART   VOLUME №1

VAULTEDITIONS.COM

. PRACTICE .
SHEET

. TATTOO .
Lettering Reference

. TYPEFACE .
MEXICANOS

DISPALY SIZE: 50^{PT} ← → **WEIGHT: REGULAR** ← → **LEADING: 74^{PT}**

LEARN MORE ABOUT
THE DESIGNER

WEBSITE: MUNTABART.COM
INSTAGRAM: MUNTAB_ART

CURATION AND RESTORATION SERVICES

© MUNTAB ART   VOLUME №1

VAULTEDITIONS.COM

.DESIGNER.
MUNTAB ART

.TATTOO.
Lettering Reference

.TYPEFACE.
MEXICANOS

DISPALY SIZE: 83ᴾᵀ ⟷ **WEIGHT: REGULAR** ⟷ **LEADING: 74ᴾᵀ**

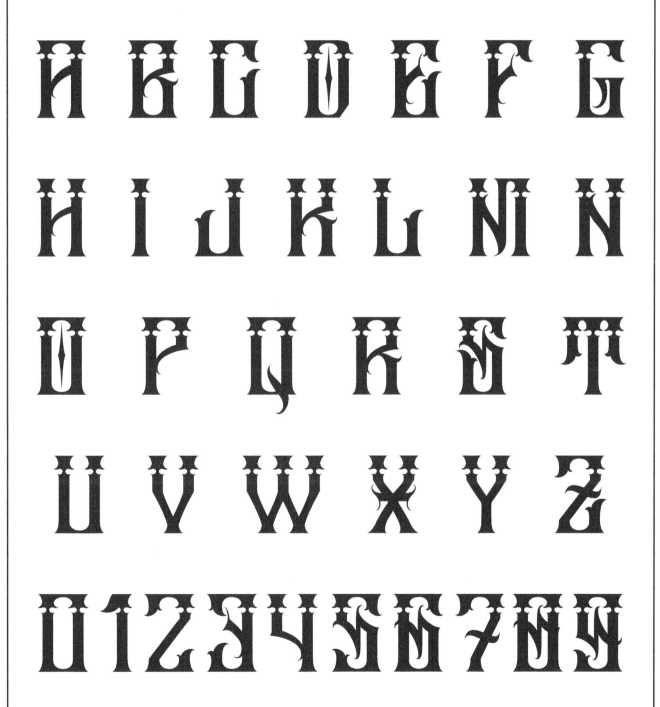

48

LEARN MORE ABOUT
THE DESIGNER

WEBSITE: MUNTABART.COM
INSTAGRAM: MUNTAB_ART

CURATION AND RESTORATION SERVICES

© MUNTAB ART

VOLUME №1

VAULTEDITIONS.COM

.PRACTICE.
SHEET

.TATTOO.
Lettering Reference

.TYPEFACE.
WESTCOAST

DISPALY SIZE: 50ᴾᵀ ← → **WEIGHT: REGULAR** ← → **LEADING: 74ᴾᵀ**

49

LEARN MORE ABOUT
THE DESIGNER

WEBSITE: MUNTABART.COM
INSTAGRAM: MUNTAB_ART

© MUNTAB ART   VOLUME Nº1

VAULTEDITIONS.COM

·DESIGNER·
MUNTAB ART

·TATTOO·
LETTERING REFERENCE

·TYPEFACE·
WESTCOAST

DISPALY SIZE: 50PT ←→ WEIGHT: REGULAR ←→ LEADING: 74PT

50

LEARN MORE ABOUT
THE DESIGNER

WEBSITE: MUNTABART.COM
INSTAGRAM: MUNTAB_ART

© MUNTAB ART | VOLUME №1

VAULTEDITIONS.COM

.PRACTICE.
SHEET

.TATTOO.
Lettering Reference

.TYPEFACE.
WESTCOAST LINE

DISPALY SIZE: 50ᴾᵀ ← → **WEIGHT: REGULAR** ← → **LEADING: 74ᴾᵀ**

LEARN MORE ABOUT
THE DESIGNER

WEBSITE: MUNTABART.COM
INSTAGRAM: MUNTAB_ART

CURATION AND RESTORATION SERVICES

© MUNTAB ART

VOLUME №1

VAULTEDITIONS.COM

.DESIGNER.
MUNTAB ART

.TATTOO.
Lettering Reference

.TYPEFACE.
WESTCOAST LINE

DISPALY SIZE: 50PT ⟷ WEIGHT: REGULAR ⟷ LEADING: 74PT

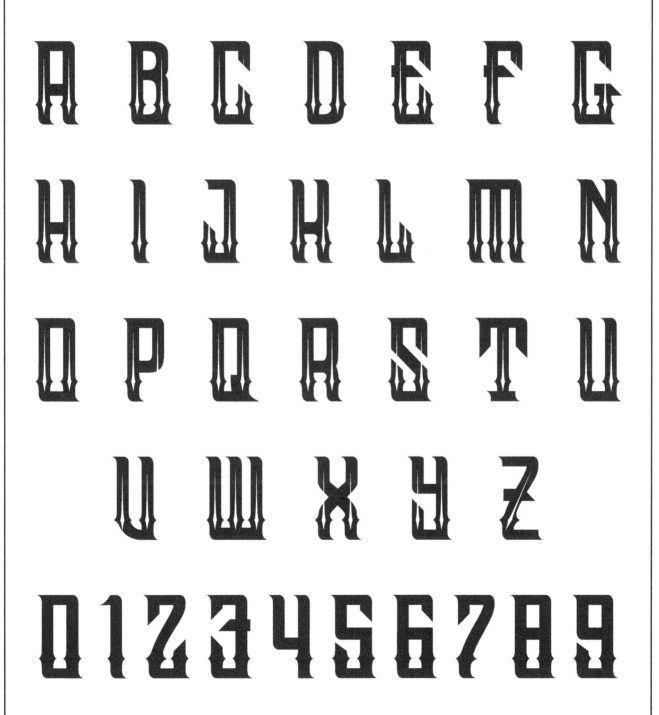

.PRACTICE.
SHEET

.TATTOO.
Lettering Reference

.TYPEFACE.
BRIGADE

DISPALY SIZE: 50^{PT} ← → WEIGHT: REGULAR ← → LEADING: 74^{PT}

LEARN MORE ABOUT
THE DESIGNER

WEBSITE: MUNTABART.COM
INSTAGRAM: MUNTAB_ART

© MUNTAB ART | VOLUME №1

VAULTEDITIONS.COM

· DESIGNER ·
MUNTAB ART

· TATTOO ·
Lettering Reference

· TYPEFACE ·
BRIGADE

DISPALY SIZE: 82ᴾᵀ ⟷ WEIGHT: REGULAR ⟷ LEADING: 74ᴾᵀ

A B C D E F

G H I J K L

M N O P Q R

S T U V W X

Y Z

0 1 2 3 4 5 6 7 8 9

LEARN MORE ABOUT
THE DESIGNER

WEBSITE: MUNTABART.COM
INSTAGRAM: MUNTAB_ART

. PRACTICE .

SHEET

. TATTOO .

Lettering Reference

. TYPEFACE .

AMSTRONG

DISPALY SIZE: 50ᴾᵀ ⟷ **WEIGHT: REGULAR** ⟷ **LEADING: 74ᴾᵀ**

.DESIGNER.
RVQ TYPE FOUNDRY

.TATTOO.
Lettering Reference

.TYPEFACE.
AMSTRONG

DISPALY SIZE: 50ᴾᵀ ⟷ WEIGHT: REGULAR ⟷ LEADING: 74ᴾᵀ

LEARN MORE ABOUT THE DESIGNER

INSTAGRAM: RVQTYPEFOUNDRY

©RVQ TYPE FOUNDRY | VOLUME №1

VAULTEDITIONS.COM

· PRACTICE ·
SHEET

· TATTOO ·
Lettering Reference

· TYPEFACE ·
AMSTRONG ORNAMENT

DISPALY SIZE: 50ᴾᵀ ← → WEIGHT: REGULAR ← → LEADING: 74ᴾᵀ

.DESIGNER.
RVQ TYPE FOUNDRY

.TATTOO.
Lettering Reference

.TYPEFACE.
AMSTRONG ORNAMENT

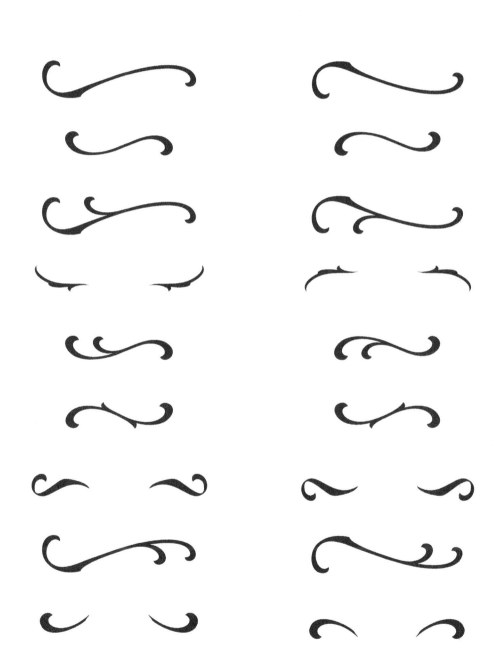

LEARN MORE ABOUT
THE DESIGNER

INSTAGRAM: RVQTYPEFOUNDRY

CURATION AND RESTORATION SERVICES

©RVQ TYPE FOUNDRY | VOLUME №1

VAULTEDITIONS.COM

.PRACTICE.
SHEET

.TATTOO.
LETTERING REFERENCE

.TYPEFACE.
ASENIA

DISPALY SIZE: 50PT ← → **WEIGHT: REGULAR** ← → **LEADING: 74**PT

.DESIGNER.
RVQ TYPE FOUNDRY

.TATTOO.
LETTERING REFERENCE

.TYPEFACE.
ASENIA

DISPALY SIZE: 54PT ← → WEIGHT: REGULAR ← → LEADING: 74PT

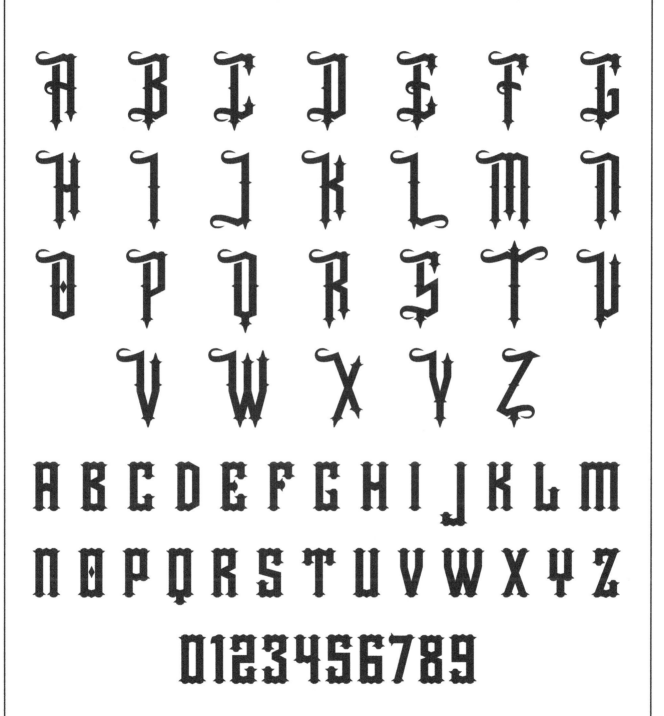

. PRACTICE .

SHEET

. TATTOO .

Lettering Reference

. TYPEFACE .

ASENIA STYLE II

DISPALY SIZE: 50ᴾᵀ ⟵⟶ **WEIGHT: REGULAR** ⟵⟶ **LEADING: 74ᴾᵀ**

61

LEARN MORE ABOUT
THE DESIGNER

INSTAGRAM: RVQTYPEFOUNDRY

©RVQ TYPE FOUNDRY

VOLUME №1

VAULTEDITIONS.COM

.DESIGNER.
RVQ TYPE FOUNDRY

.TATTOO.
Lettering Reference

.TYPEFACE.
ASENIA STYLE II

DISPALY SIZE: 66ᴾᵀ ←→ **WEIGHT: REGULAR** ←→ **LEADING: 74ᴾᵀ**

A B C D E F G

H I J K L M N

O P Q R S T U

V W X Y Z

a b c d e f g h i j k l m

n o p q r s t u v w x y z

0 1 2 3 4 5 6 7 8 9

62

LEARN MORE ABOUT
THE DESIGNER

INSTAGRAM: RVQTYPEFOUNDRY

CURATION AND RESTORATION SERVICES

©RVQ TYPE FOUNDRY

VOLUME №1

VAULTEDITIONS.COM

.PRACTICE.
SHEET

.TATTOO.
Lettering Reference

.TYPEFACE.
ASENIA STYLE III

DISPALY SIZE: 50PT ⟷ WEIGHT: REGULAR ⟷ LEADING: 74PT

.DESIGNER.
RVQ TYPE FOUNDRY

.TATTOO.
Lettering Reference

.TYPEFACE.
ASENIA STYLE III

DISPALY SIZE: 66ᴾᵀ ⟷ **WEIGHT: REGULAR** ⟷ **LEADING: 74ᴾᵀ**

A B C D E F G

H I J K L M N

O P Q R S T U

V W X Y Z

a b c d e f g h i j k l m

n o p q r s t u v w x y z

0 1 2 3 4 5 6 7 8 9

64

LEARN MORE ABOUT
THE DESIGNER

INSTAGRAM: RVQTYPEFOUNDRY

CURATION AND RESTORATION SERVICES

©RVQ TYPE FOUNDRY | VOLUME №1

VAULTEDITIONS.COM

. PRACTICE .

SHEET

. TATTOO .

Lettering Reference

. TYPEFACE .

BLACK VISION

DISPALY SIZE: 50ᴾᵀ ⟷ WEIGHT: REGULAR ⟷ LEADING: 74ᴾᵀ

65

LEARN MORE ABOUT
THE DESIGNER

INSTAGRAM: RVQTYPEFOUNDRY

©RVQ TYPE FOUNDRY

VOLUME №1

VAULTEDITIONS.COM

. DESIGNER .
RVQ TYPE FOUNDRY

. TATTOO .
Lettering Reference

. TYPEFACE .
BLACK VISION

DISPALY SIZE: 96ᴾᵀ ⟷ WEIGHT: REGULAR ⟷ LEADING: 74ᴾᵀ

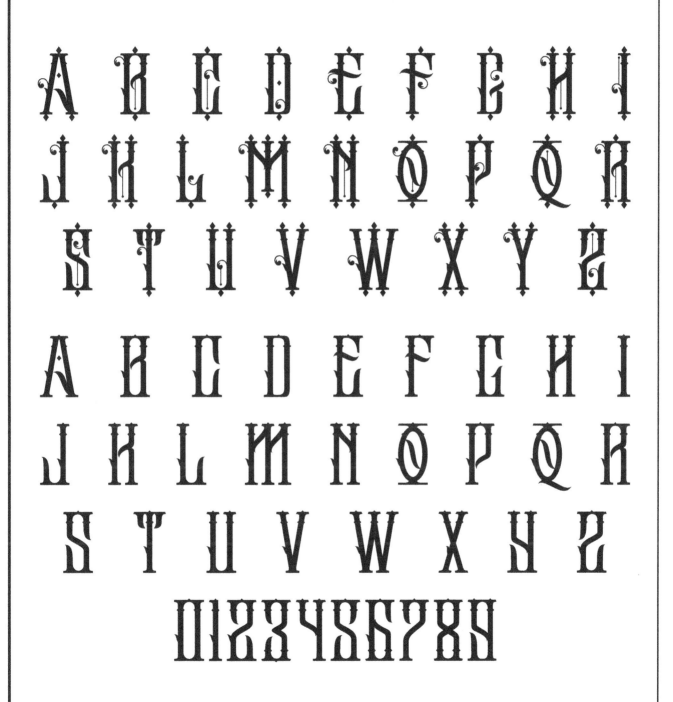

.PRACTICE.
SHEET

.TATTOO.
Lettering Reference

.TYPEFACE.
CALIFORNIA FREESTYLE

DISPALY SIZE: 50PT ⟷ **WEIGHT: REGULAR** ⟷ **LEADING: 74PT**

.DESIGNER.
RVQ TYPE FOUNDRY

.TATTOO.
Lettering Reference

.TYPEFACE.
CALIFORNIA FREESTYLE

DISPALY SIZE: 68ᴾᵀ ←→ **WEIGHT: REGULAR** ←→ **LEADING: 74ᴾᵀ**

·PRACTICE·
SHEET

·TATTOO·
Lettering Reference

·TYPEFACE·
CALIFORNIA SWASH

DISPALY SIZE: 50^{PT}   WEIGHT: REGULAR   LEADING: 74^{PT}

69

LEARN MORE ABOUT
THE DESIGNER

INSTAGRAM: RVQTYPEFOUNDRY

CURATION AND RESTORATION SERVICE

©RVQ TYPE FOUNDRY   VOLUME №1

VAULTEDITIONS.COM

.DESIGNER.
RVQ TYPE FOUNDRY

.TATTOO.
Lettering Reference

.TYPEFACE.
CALIFORNIA SWASH

DISPALY SIZE: 90ᴾᵀ   ⟵————⟶   WEIGHT: REGULAR   ⟵————⟶   LEADING: 74ᴾᵀ

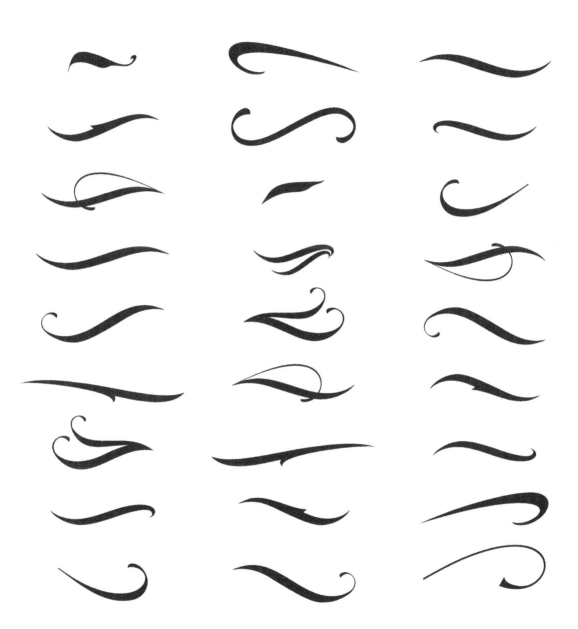

70

LEARN MORE ABOUT
THE DESIGNER

INSTAGRAM: RVQTYPEFOUNDRY

CURATION AND RESTORATION SERVICES

©RVQ TYPE FOUNDRY   VOLUME №1

VAULTEDITIONS.COM

.PRACTICE.
SHEET

.TATTOO.
Lettering Reference

.TYPEFACE.
NEW CAPRICORN

DISPALY SIZE: 50ᴾᵀ ← → **WEIGHT: REGULAR** ← → **LEADING: 74ᴾᵀ**

·DESIGNER·
RVQ TYPE FOUNDRY

·TATTOO·
Lettering Reference

·TYPEFACE·
NEW CAPRICORN

DISPALY SIZE: 50ᴾᵀ ⟷ **WEIGHT: REGULAR** ⟷ **LEADING: 74ᴾᵀ**

·PRACTICE·
SHEET

·TATTOO·
Lettering Reference

·TYPEFACE·
RIOTIC

·DESIGNER·
RVQ TYPE FOUNDRY

·TATTOO·
Lettering Reference

·TYPEFACE·
RIOTIC

DISPALY SIZE: 79ᴾᵀ ⟷ WEIGHT: REGULAR ⟷ LEADING: 74ᴾᵀ

A B C D E F
G H I J K
L M N O P
Q R S T U
V W X Y Z

0 1 2 3 4 5 6 7 8 9

.PRACTICE.
SHEET

.TATTOO.
Lettering Reference

.TYPEFACE.
THE MARIAM STORY

DISPALY SIZE: 50ᴾᵀ ⟵⟶ WEIGHT: REGULAR ⟵⟶ LEADING: 74ᴾᵀ

· DESIGNER ·
RVQ TYPE FOUNDRY

· TATTOO ·
Lettering Reference

· TYPEFACE ·
THE MARIAM STORY

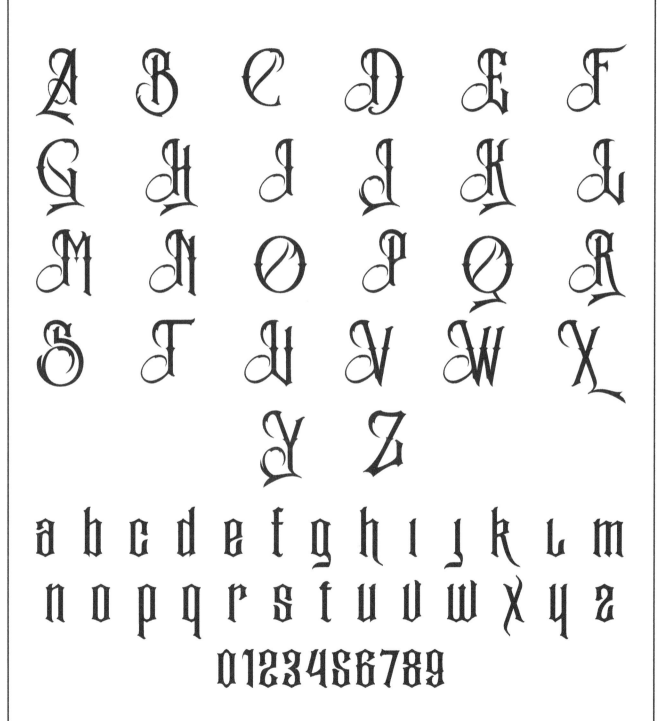

LEARN MORE ABOUT
THE DESIGNER

INSTAGRAM: RVQTYPEFOUNDRY

CURATION AND RESTORATION SERVICES

©RVQ TYPE FOUNDRY — VOLUME №1

VAULTEDITIONS.COM

.PRACTICE.

SHEET

.TATTOO.

Lettering Reference

.TYPEFACE.

WEDNESDAY

DISPALY SIZE: 50ᴾᵀ ← → WEIGHT: REGULAR ← → LEADING: 74ᴾᵀ

LEARN MORE ABOUT
THE DESIGNER

INSTAGRAM: RVQTYPEFOUNDRY

©RVQ TYPE FOUNDRY

VOLUME №1

VAULTEDITIONS.COM

. DESIGNER .
RVQ TYPE FOUNDRY

. TATTOO .
Lettering Reference

. TYPEFACE .
WEDNESDAY

DISPALY SIZE: 75PT ⟵⟶ **WEIGHT: REGULAR** ⟵⟶ **LEADING: 74PT**

·PRACTICE·
SHEET

·TATTOO·
LETTERING REFERENCE

·TYPEFACE·
NORTHERN

DISPALY SIZE: 50PT ← → **WEIGHT: REGULAR** ← → **LEADING: 74**PT

LEARN MORE ABOUT
THE DESIGNER

INSTAGRAM: RVQTYPEFOUNDRY

©RVQ TYPE FOUNDRY | VOLUME №1

VAULTEDITIONS.COM

. DESIGNER .
RVQ TYPE FOUNDRY

. TATTOO .
Lettering Reference

. TYPEFACE .
NORTHERN

DISPALY SIZE: 50PT ⟷ **WEIGHT: REGULAR** ⟷ **LEADING: 74PT**

.PRACTICE.
SHEET

.TATTOO.
Lettering Reference

.TYPEFACE.
NORTHERN ORNAMENT

DISPALY SIZE: 50ᴾᵀ ← → **WEIGHT: REGULAR** ← → **LEADING: 74ᴾᵀ**

.DESIGNER.
RVQ TYPE FOUNDRY

.TATTOO.
LETTERING REFERENCE

.TYPEFACE.
NORTHERN ORNAMENT

DISPALY SIZE: 50ᴾᵀ ⟷ **WEIGHT: REGULAR** ⟷ **LEADING: 74ᴾᵀ**

.PRACTICE.
SHEET

.TATTOO.
LETTERING REFERENCE

.TYPEFACE.
SECTIONE BRIGHT SCRIPT

DISPALY SIZE: 50^{PT} ⟷ WEIGHT: REGULAR ⟷ LEADING: 74^{PT}

83

LEARN MORE ABOUT
THE DESIGNER

INSTAGRAM: RVQTYPEFOUNDRY

CURATION AND RESTORATION SERVICES

©RVQ TYPE FOUNDRY | VOLUME №1

VAULTEDITIONS.COM

· DESIGNER ·
RVQ TYPE FOUNDRY

· TATTOO ·
LETTERING REFERENCE

· TYPEFACE ·
SECTIONE BRIGHT SCRIPT

DISPALY SIZE: 81ᴾᵀ ⟷ **WEIGHT: REGULAR** ⟷ **LEADING: 74ᴾᵀ**

A B C D E F G H

I J K L M N O P Q

R S T U V W X Y Z

a b c d e f g h i j k l m

n o p q r s t u v w x y z

0 1 2 3 4 5 6 7 8 9

.PRACTICE.
SHEET

.TATTOO.
LETTERING REFERENCE

.TYPEFACE.
SECTIONE BRIGHT SWASH

DISPALY SIZE: 50ᴾᵀ ⟷ **WEIGHT: REGULAR** ⟷ **LEADING: 74ᴾᵀ**

.DESIGNER.
RVQ TYPE FOUNDRY

.TATTOO.
LETTERING REFERENCE

.TYPEFACE.
SECTIONE BRIGHT SWASH

DISPALY SIZE: 81ᴾᵀ ← → WEIGHT: REGULAR ← → LEADING: 74ᴾᵀ

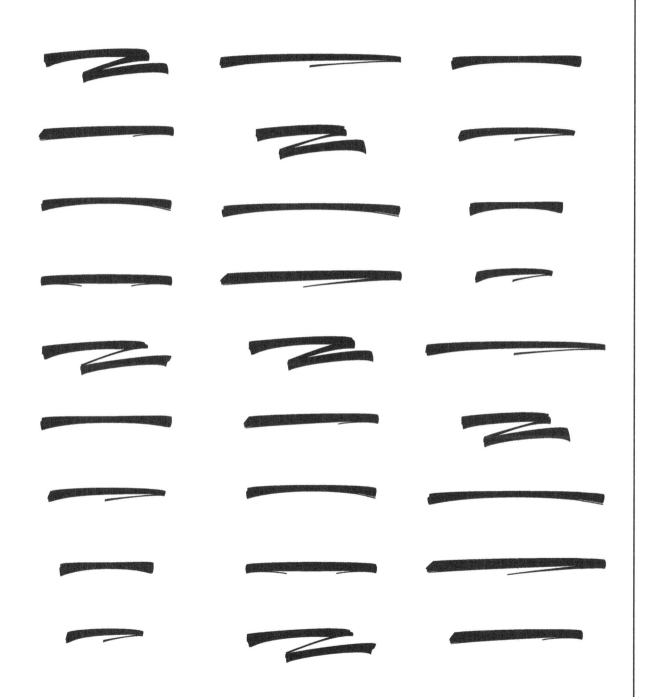

.PRACTICE.
SHEET

.TATTOO.
Lettering Reference

.TYPEFACE.
BARUNA

DISPALY SIZE: 50ᴾᵀ ⟷ **WEIGHT: REGULAR** ⟷ **LEADING: 74ᴾᵀ**

87

LEARN MORE ABOUT
THE DESIGNER

WEBSITE: CREATIVEMEDIALAB.NET
INSTAGRAM: @CREATIVEMEDIALAB
FACEBOOK: FB.COM/MYCREATIVEMEDIALAB
TWITTER: @CREATIVEMEDIALAB

©HADEH MAHARDIHA

VOLUME №1

VAULTEDITIONS.COM

·DESIGNER·
CREATIVEMEDIALAB

·TATTOO·
LETTERING REFERENCE

·TYPEFACE·
BARUNA

DISPALY SIZE: 57ᴾᵀ ←→ WEIGHT: REGULAR ←→ LEADING: 74ᴾᵀ

A B C D E F G H I J

K L M N O P Q R S

T U V W X Y Z

a b c d e f g h i j k l m

n o p q r s t u v w x y z

0 1 2 3 4 5 6 7 8 9

LEARN MORE ABOUT
THE DESIGNER

WEBSITE: CREATIVEMEDIALAB.NET
INSTAGRAM: @CREATIVEMEDIALAB
FACEBOOK: FB.COM/MYCREATIVEMEDIALAB
TWITTER: @CREATIVEMEDIALAB

©HADEH MAHARDIKA

VOLUME №1

VAULTEDITIONS.COM

. PRACTICE .

SHEET

. TATTOO .

Lettering Reference

. TYPEFACE .

BARUNA ORNAMENTS

DISPALY SIZE: 50ᴾᵀ ← → **WEIGHT: REGULAR** ← → **LEADING: 74ᴾᵀ**

LEARN MORE ABOUT
THE DESIGNER

WEBSITE: CREATIVEMEDIALAB.NET
INSTAGRAM: @CREATIVEMEDIALAB
FACEBOOK: FB.COM/MYCREATIVEMEDIALAB
TWITTER: @CREATIVEMEDIALAB

© HADEH MAHARDIHA

VOLUME №1

VAULTEDITIONS.COM

.DESIGNER.
CREATIVEMEDIALAB

.TATTOO.
LETTERING REFERENCE

.TYPEFACE.
BARUNA ORNAMENTS

DISPALY SIZE: 57PT ←→ **WEIGHT: REGULAR** ←→ **LEADING: 74PT**

90

**LEARN MORE ABOUT
THE DESIGNER**

WEBSITE: CREATIVEMEDIALAB.NET
INSTAGRAM: @CREATIVEMEDIALAB
FACEBOOK: FB.COM/MYCREATIVEMEDIALAB
TWITTER: @CREATIVEMEDIALAB

©RVQ TYPE FOUNDRY   VOLUME №1

VAULTEDITIONS.COM

.PRACTICE.
SHEET

.TATTOO.
Lettering Reference

.TYPEFACE.
BASELARD

DISPALY SIZE: 50^{PT} ⟷ **WEIGHT: REGULAR** ⟷ **LEADING: 74^{PT}**

91

LEARN MORE ABOUT
THE DESIGNER

WEBSITE: CREATIVEMEDIALAB.NET
INSTAGRAM: @CREATIVEMEDIALAB
FACEBOOK: FB.COM/MYCREATIVEMEDIALAB
TWITTER: @CREATIVEMEDIALAB

©HADEH MAHARDIHA

VOLUME №1

VAULTEDITIONS.COM

.DESIGNER.
CREATIVEMEDIALAB

.TATTOO.
LETTERING REFERENCE

.TYPEFACE.
BASELARD

DISPALY SIZE: 60ᴾᵀ ⟷ WEIGHT: REGULAR ⟷ LEADING: 74ᴾᵀ

A B C D E F G H I
J K L M N O P Q R
S T U V W X Y Z

a b c d e f g h i j k l m
n o p q r s t u v w x y z
0 1 2 3 4 5 6 7 8 9

LEARN MORE ABOUT
THE DESIGNER

WEBSITE: CREATIVEMEDIALAB.NET
INSTAGRAM: @CREATIVEMEDIALAB
FACEBOOK: FB.COM/MYCREATIVEMEDIALAB
TWITTER: @CREATIVEMEDIALAB

©HADEH MAHARDIKA VOLUME №1

VAULTEDITIONS.COM

.PRACTICE.
SHEET

.TATTOO.
Lettering Reference

.TYPEFACE.
BASELARD ORNAMENT

DISPALY SIZE: 50ᴾᵀ ⟷ WEIGHT: REGULAR ⟷ LEADING: 74ᴾᵀ

LEARN MORE ABOUT
THE DESIGNER

WEBSITE: CREATIVEMEDIALAB.NET
INSTAGRAM: @CREATIVEMEDIALAB
FACEBOOK: FB.COM/MYCREATIVEMEDIALAB
TWITTER: @CREATIVEMEDIALAB

.DESIGNER.
CREATIVEMEDIALAB

.TATTOO.
LETTERING REFERENCE

.TYPEFACE.
BASELARD ORNAMENT

DISPALY SIZE: 50ᴾᵀ ←→ WEIGHT: REGULAR ←→ LEADING: 74ᴾᵀ

LEARN MORE ABOUT THE DESIGNER

WEBSITE: CREATIVEMEDIALAB.NET
INSTAGRAM: @CREATIVEMEDIALAB
FACEBOOK: FB.COM/MYCREATIVEMEDIALAB
TWITTER: @CREATIVEMEDIALAB

CREATION AND RESTORATION SERVICES CURATION

©HADEH MAHARDIHA | VOLUME №1

VAULTEDITIONS.COM

.PRACTICE.
SHEET

.TATTOO.
Lettering Reference

.TYPEFACE.
BLACK CAMEO

DISPALY SIZE: 50^{PT} ⟷ WEIGHT: REGULAR ⟷ LEADING: 74^{PT}

.DESIGNER.
CREATIVEMEDIALAB

.TATTOO.
Lettering Reference

.TYPEFACE.
BLACK CAMEO

DISPLAY SIZE: 70ᴾᵀ ⟵⟶ WEIGHT: REGULAR ⟵⟶ LEADING: 74ᴾᵀ

A B C D E F G H I J
K L M N O P Q R S
T U V W X Y Z

a b c d e f g h i j k l m n o
p q r s t u v w x y z
0 1 2 3 4 5 6 7 8 9

LEARN MORE ABOUT
THE DESIGNER

WEBSITE: CREATIVEMEDIALAB.NET
INSTAGRAM: @CREATIVEMEDIALAB
FACEBOOK: FB.COM/MYCREATIVEMEDIALAB
TWITTER: @CREATIVEMEDIALAB

CREATION AND RESTORATION SERVICES CURATION

©HADEH MAHARDIKA | VOLUME №1

VAULTEDITIONS.COM

.PRACTICE.
SHEET

.TATTOO.
Lettering Reference

.TYPEFACE.
BLACK CAMEO SWASH

DISPALY SIZE: 50ᴾᵀ ← → **WEIGHT: REGULAR** ← → **LEADING: 74ᴾᵀ**

**LEARN MORE ABOUT
THE DESIGNER**

WEBSITE: CREATIVEMEDIALAB.NET
INSTAGRAM: @CREATIVEMEDIALAB
FACEBOOK: FB.COM/MYCREATIVEMEDIALAB
TWITTER: @CREATIVEMEDIALAB

CURATION AND RESTORATION SERVICES

©HADEH MAHARDIHA

VOLUME №1

VAULTEDITIONS.COM

.DESIGNER.
CREATIVEMEDIALAB

.TATTOO.
Lettering Reference

.TYPEFACE.
BLACK CAMEO SWASH

DISPALY SIZE: 50ᴾᵀ ⟷ WEIGHT: REGULAR ⟷ LEADING: 74ᴾᵀ

LEARN MORE ABOUT
THE DESIGNER

WEBSITE: CREATIVEMEDIALAB.NET
INSTAGRAM: @CREATIVEMEDIALAB
FACEBOOK: FB.COM/MYCREATIVEMEDIALAB
TWITTER: @CREATIVEMEDIALAB

©HADEH MAHARDIHA | VOLUME №1

VAULTEDITIONS.COM

.PRACTICE.
SHEET

.TATTOO.
Lettering Reference

.TYPEFACE.
CARPELLON

DISPALY SIZE: 50ᴾᵀ ⟷ WEIGHT: REGULAR ⟷ LEADING: 74ᴾᵀ

99

LEARN MORE ABOUT
THE DESIGNER

WEBSITE: CREATIVEMEDIALAB.NET
INSTAGRAM: @CREATIVEMEDIALAB
FACEBOOK: FB.COM/MYCREATIVEMEDIALAB
TWITTER: @CREATIVEMEDIALAB

CURATION AND RESTORATION SERVICES

©HADEH MAHARDIHA

VOLUME №1

VAULTEDITIONS.COM

.DESIGNER.
CREATIVEMEDIALAB

.TATTOO.
Lettering Reference

.TYPEFACE.
CARPELLON

DISPLAY SIZE: 50PT ←——→ **WEIGHT: REGULAR** ←——→ **LEADING: 74PT**

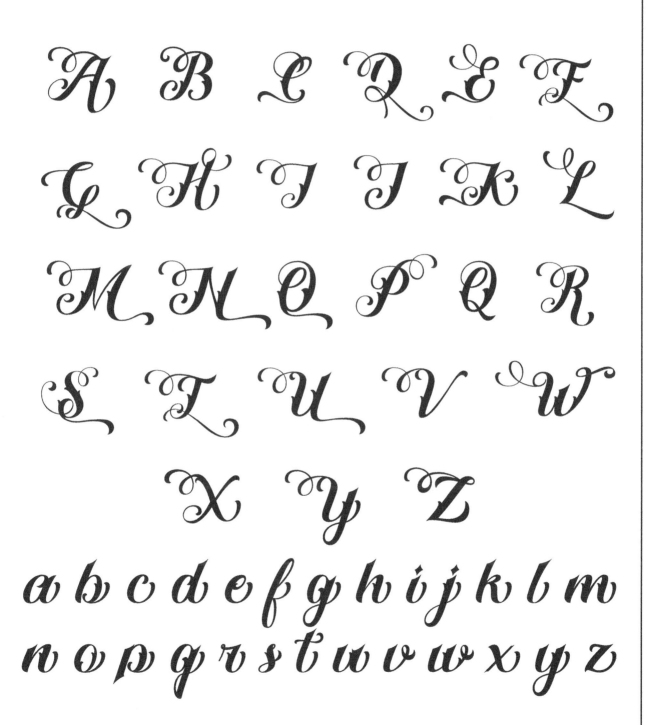

100

LEARN MORE ABOUT
THE DESIGNER

WEBSITE: CREATIVEMEDIALAB.NET
INSTAGRAM: @CREATIVEMEDIALAB
FACEBOOK: FB.COM/MYCREATIVEMEDIALAB
TWITTER: @CREATIVEMEDIALAB

CURATION AND RESTORATION SERVICES

©HADEH MAHARDIKA | VOLUME №1

VAULTEDITIONS.COM

.PRACTICE.
SHEET

.TATTOO.
Lettering Reference

.TYPEFACE.
CARPELLON ORNAMENT

DISPALY SIZE: 50ᴾᵀ ⟷ **WEIGHT: REGULAR** ⟷ **LEADING: 74ᴾᵀ**

101

LEARN MORE ABOUT
THE DESIGNER

WEBSITE: CREATIVEMEDIALAB.NET
INSTAGRAM: @CREATIVEMEDIALAB
FACEBOOK: FB.COM/MYCREATIVEMEDIALAB
TWITTER: @CREATIVEMEDIALAB

©HADEH MAHARDIHA   VOLUME №1

VAULTEDITIONS.COM

.DESIGNER.
CREATIVEMEDIALAB

.TATTOO.
Lettering Reference

.TYPEFACE.
CARPELLON ORNAMENT

DISPALY SIZE: 50ᴾᵀ ⟷ **WEIGHT: REGULAR** ⟷ **LEADING: 74ᴾᵀ**

LEARN MORE ABOUT THE DESIGNER

WEBSITE: CREATIVEMEDIALAB.NET
INSTAGRAM: @CREATIVEMEDIALAB
FACEBOOK: FB.COM/MYCREATIVEMEDIALAB
TWITTER: @CREATIVEMEDIALAB

CURATION AND RESTORATION SERVICES

©HADEH MAHARDIHA | VOLUME №1

VAULTEDITIONS.COM

.PRACTICE.
SHEET

.TATTOO.
Lettering Reference

.TYPEFACE.
CATTERDALE

DISPALY SIZE: 50^{PT} ← → WEIGHT: REGULAR ← → LEADING: 74^{PT}

LEARN MORE ABOUT
THE DESIGNER

WEBSITE: CREATIVEMEDIALAB.NET
INSTAGRAM: @CREATIVEMEDIALAB
FACEBOOK: FB.COM/MYCREATIVEMEDIALAB
TWITTER: @CREATIVEMEDIALAB

CURATION AND RESTORATION SERVICES

©HADEH MAHARDIHA

VOLUME №1

VAULTEDITIONS.COM

·DESIGNER·
CREATIVEMEDIALAB

·TATTOO·
Lettering Reference

·TYPEFACE·
CATTERDALE

DISPALY SIZE: 63PT ⟷ **WEIGHT: REGULAR** ⟷ **LEADING: 74PT**

A B C D E F G
H I J K L M N O
P Q R S T U V
W X Y Z

a b c d e f g h i j k l m n
o p q r s t u v w x y z
0 1 2 3 4 5 6 7 8 9

104

LEARN MORE ABOUT
THE DESIGNER

WEBSITE: CREATIVEMEDIALAB.NET
INSTAGRAM: @CREATIVEMEDIALAB
FACEBOOK: FB.COM/MYCREATIVEMEDIALAB
TWITTER: @CREATIVEMEDIALAB

.PRACTICE.
SHEET

.TATTOO.
Lettering Reference

.TYPEFACE.
CATTERDALE ORNAMENT

DISPALY SIZE: 50^{PT} ⟷ **WEIGHT: REGULAR** ⟷ **LEADING: 74^{PT}**

LEARN MORE ABOUT THE DESIGNER

WEBSITE: CREATIVEMEDIALAB.NET
INSTAGRAM: @CREATIVEMEDIALAB
FACEBOOK: FB.COM/MYCREATIVEMEDIALAB
TWITTER: @CREATIVEMEDIALAB

©HADEK MAHARDIKA

VOLUME №1

VAULTEDITIONS.COM

.DESIGNER.
CREATIVEMEDIALAB

.TATTOO.
LETTERING REFERENCE

.TYPEFACE.
CATTERDALE ORNAMENT

DISPALY SIZE: 50ᴾᵀ ⟷ **WEIGHT: REGULAR** ⟷ **LEADING: 63ᴾᵀ**

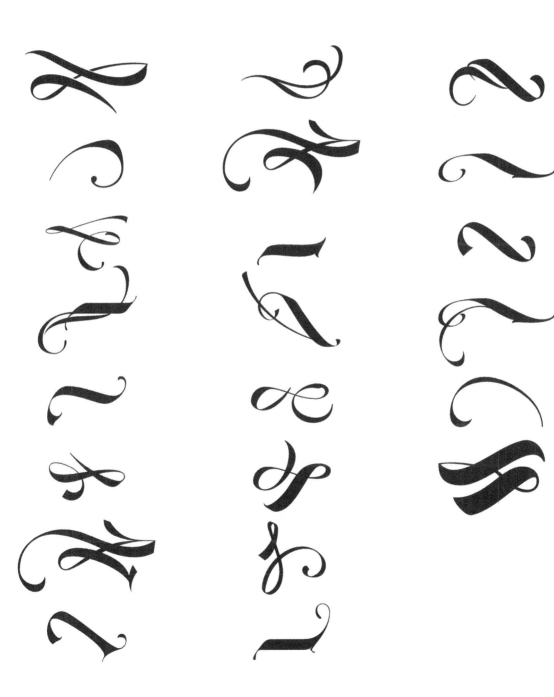

LEARN MORE ABOUT THE DESIGNER

WEBSITE: CREATIVEMEDIALAB.NET
INSTAGRAM: @CREATIVEMEDIALAB
FACEBOOK: FB.COM/MYCREATIVEMEDIALAB
TWITTER: @CREATIVEMEDIALAB

©HADEH MAHARDIHA

VOLUME №1

VAULTEDITIONS.COM

.PRACTICE.
SHEET

.TATTOO.
Lettering Reference

.TYPEFACE.
LORDISH

DISPALY SIZE: 50PT ← → **WEIGHT: REGULAR** ← → **LEADING: 74**PT

107

LEARN MORE ABOUT
THE DESIGNER

WEBSITE: CREATIVEMEDIALAB.NET
INSTAGRAM: @CREATIVEMEDIALAB
FACEBOOH: FB.COM/MYCREATIVEMEDIALAB
TWITTER: @CREATIVEMEDIALAB

©HADEH MAHARDIHA

VOLUME №1

VAULTEDITIONS.COM

.DESIGNER.
CREATIVEMEDIALAB

.TATTOO.
Lettering Reference

.TYPEFACE.
LORDISH

DISPALY SIZE: 60ᴾᵀ ⟷ WEIGHT: REGULAR ⟷ LEADING: 74ᴾᵀ

LEARN MORE ABOUT
THE DESIGNER

WEBSITE: CREATIVEMEDIALAB.NET
INSTAGRAM: @CREATIVEMEDIALAB
FACEBOOH: FB.COM/MYCREATIVEMEDIALAB
TWITTER: @CREATIVEMEDIALAB

.PRACTICE.
SHEET

.TATTOO.
Lettering Reference

.TYPEFACE.
LORDISH

DISPALY SIZE: 50ᴾᵀ ⟵⟶ **WEIGHT: THIN** ⟵⟶ **LEADING: 74ᴾᵀ**

**LEARN MORE ABOUT
THE DESIGNER**

WEBSITE: CREATIVEMEDIALAB.NET
INSTAGRAM: @CREATIVEMEDIALAB
FACEBOOK: FB.COM/MYCREATIVEMEDIALAB
TWITTER: @CREATIVEMEDIALAB

©HADEH MAHARDIHA **VOLUME №1**

VAULTEDITIONS.COM

.DESIGNER.
CREATIVEMEDIALAB

.TATTOO.
Lettering Reference

.TYPEFACE.
LORDISH

DISPALY SIZE: 60ᴾᵀ ⟷ **WEIGHT: THIN** ⟷ **LEADING: 74ᴾᵀ**

LEARN MORE ABOUT
THE DESIGNER

WEBSITE: CREATIVEMEDIALAB.NET
INSTAGRAM: @CREATIVEMEDIALAB
FACEBOOK: FB.COM/MYCREATIVEMEDIALAB
TWITTER: @CREATIVEMEDIALAB

©HADEH MAHARDIHA | VOLUME №1

VAULTEDITIONS.COM

.PRACTICE.
SHEET

.TATTOO.
Lettering Reference

.TYPEFACE.
RAJJAH FAMILLIA

DISPLAY SIZE: 50ᴾᵀ ⟷ **WEIGHT: REGULAR** ⟷ **LEADING: 74ᴾᵀ**

LEARN MORE ABOUT THE DESIGNER

WEBSITE: CREATIVEMEDIALAB.NET
INSTAGRAM: @CREATIVEMEDIALAB
FACEBOOK: FB.COM/MYCREATIVEMEDIALAB
TWITTER: @CREATIVEMEDIALAB

©HADEH MAHARDIHA | VOLUME №1

.DESIGNER.
CREATIVEMEDIALAB

.TATTOO.
Lettering Reference

.TYPEFACE.
RAJJAH FAMILLIA

DISPALY SIZE: 50ᴾᵀ ⟵ ⟶ WEIGHT: BOLD ⟵ ⟶ LEADING: 74ᴾᵀ

112

LEARN MORE ABOUT
THE DESIGNER

WEBSITE: CREATIVEMEDIALAB.NET
INSTAGRAM: @CREATIVEMEDIALAB
FACEBOOK: FB.COM/MYCREATIVEMEDIALAB
TWITTER: @CREATIVEMEDIALAB

©HADEH MAHARDIHA

VOLUME №1

VAULTEDITIONS.COM

.PRACTICE.
SHEET

.TATTOO.
Lettering Reference

.TYPEFACE.
YELLOST

DISPALY SIZE: 50ᴾᵀ ⟷ **WEIGHT: REGULAR** ⟷ **LEADING: 74ᴾᵀ**

113

LEARN MORE ABOUT
THE DESIGNER

WEBSITE: CREATIVEMEDIALAB.NET
INSTAGRAM: @CREATIVEMEDIALAB
FACEBOOK: FB.COM/MYCREATIVEMEDIALAB
TWITTER: @CREATIVEMEDIALAB

©HADEH MAHARDIHA   VOLUME №1

VAULTEDITIONS.COM

.DESIGNER.
CREATIVEMEDIALAB

.TATTOO.
Lettering Reference

.TYPEFACE.
YELLOST

DISPALY SIZE: 50PT ⟷ WEIGHT: REGULAR ⟷ LEADING: 74PT

A B C D E F G H I
J K L M N O P Q R
S T U V W X Y Z

A B C D E F G H I J K L M N
O P Q R S T U V W X Y Z
0 1 2 3 4 5 6 7 8 9

114

LEARN MORE ABOUT
THE DESIGNER

WEBSITE: CREATIVEMEDIALAB.NET
INSTAGRAM: @CREATIVEMEDIALAB
FACEBOOK: FB.COM/MYCREATIVEMEDIALAB
TWITTER: @CREATIVEMEDIALAB

©HADEK MAHARDIHA

VOLUME №1

VAULTEDITIONS.COM

LEARN MORE

At Vault Editions, our mission is to create the world's most diverse and comprehensive collection of image archives available for artists, designers and curious minds. If you have enjoyed this book, you can find more of our titles available at vaulteditions.com.

REVIEW THIS BOOK

As a small, family-owned independent publisher, reviews help spread the word about our work. We would be incredibly grateful if you could leave an honest review of this title wherever you purchased this book.

JOIN OUR COMMUNITY

Are you a creative and curious individual? If so, you will love our community on Instagram. Every day we share bizarre and beautiful artwork ranging from 17th and 18th-century natural history and scientific illustration, to mythical beasts, ornamental designs, anatomical illustration and more. Join our community of 100K+ people today— search @vault_editions on Instagram.

DOWNLOAD YOUR FILES

STEP ONE

Enter the following web address in your web browser on a desktop computer.

www.vaulteditions.com/tli

STEP TWO

Enter the following unique password to access the download page.

tli38473fsdrv2

STEP THREE

Follow the prompts to access your high-resolution files.

TECHNICAL ASSISTANCE

For all technical assistance, please email: info@vaulteditions.com

VAULTEDITIONS.COM

Made in the USA
Monee, IL
17 September 2023

42893052R00066